GU00832859

Wakefield Press

LONNIE'S LAMENT

Thoughtful—and yet forgetful, easily distracted, hardly there sometimes—Ken Bolton's is a lyrical figure limned against the harsh outlines, the stark colours, of the Adelaide art world, adding a word here, a thought there, in the general flux of words and deeds around town. A zany, he was for a long time employed at Adelaide's Experimental Art Foundation. He edits Little Esther books.

LONNIE'S LAMENT

TOWARDS A HISTORY OF THE VANISHING PRESENT

KEN BOLTON

Wakefield
Press

Wakefield Press
16 Rose Street
Mile End
South Australia 5031
www.wakefieldpress.com.au

First published 2017

Cover designed by M. Grimm
Cover illustration: 'Interior with Krazy Kat', by Howard Climbing
Typeset by Michael Deves, Wakefield Press

National Library of Australia Cataloguing-in-Publication entry

Creator: Bolton, Ken, 1949– , author.
Title: Lonnie's lament / Ken Bolton.
ISBN: 978 1 74305 472 7 (paperback).
Subjects: Australian poetry.

CORIOLE

McLAREN VALE

"ALL NEW TUNES
ON JUKEBOX"

— red biro, on cardboard,
back room of the 'Nag's Head',
Forest Lodge, summer, 1977

Many thanks to the editors for publishing these poems:

'Brief Life' appeared in *Best Australian Poems* 2010

'The Funnies' in *steamer* magazine and *Best Australian Poems* 2011

'Train Tripping', '2.12.08 – Poem for Philip Whalen', 'New Way of Worrying',
and 'What's Best' in *JACKET2*

'30.11.12' in *Australian Book Review*

'Spirits' and 'September Postcards' in *Otoliths*

'A Review' in *Shearsman* (UK)
and 'Maybe For You' in *Shampoo*

CONTENTS

I

II

III

IV
(ALL NEW TUNES)

I

2/12/08 — A Poem For Philip Whalen

"Here it comes again, imagination of myself"
Philip Whalen, 'International Date Line, Monday / Monday 27:IX:67'

Here it comes again, imagination of myself:
I sit, in the harsh light, in a study
(mine)

It's the light I like,
& it's late.

"In a study" always suggests "He was in
a bad mood, tense with it"—not that—
reading Whalen, a book of drawings by Kirchner,

the Berlin Street Scenes—in an attempt
to gain *some* purchase, kick off
from something different—thinking

of Yuri, a bit, Cath's eldest son, the one
I know least but like & like his difficult life
& how he's dealt with it. *"Yuri—I will speak*

with you later!" My friends the poets, famous,
in their way—in the not very satisfying way available
to them (some)—large in my mind at any rate—

& another, rather foolish, at the same time as
rather good—well, alternately, from poem to poem—
something of a comeback. Another friend, ill

seriously mortally time running out. How quickly? How
quickly for all of us, the question. ('A' question.) Anna, &
boyfriend Chris, on their anger at / fascination with

The Howard Years documentary a
self-serving account but, as they say, so far
the major & lone political fact of their lives

It will be their early history: *yech*—Reith,
Howard himself (whom I never expected
in the 80s I would have to hate—what future

did *he* have?). The rest.
'Consigned' now 'to oblivion'—to echo & re-echo
in succeeding waves

of revision, counter-construal,

like analyses of the Third Republic, the French
Second Empire. Where are we now? Even 'interesting times'
seem to follow a pattern—the bangs & whimpers

louder, more ironically conventional for their
inadequacy to the occasion. Will America go under
because of Bush? how appropriate

But was that my point? Late at night,
not even worrying. Whalen ... the Kirchner drawings.

Go under? What,
next week?

Okay, then.

"It may never happen!" Isn't that the joke?

If it takes ten years, if it takes twenty,
it will be cataclysmic. Tho—(20 years)—

I might be out of the way—or less concerned by then.
If curious as to the outcomes. For
twenty years —for thirty— amused

—"amused at best"—

by Whalen's politics—when I thought of them—
the raves & rants, observations,
of a hippy dropout. Well, a Beat

the one I like best. What did Whalen change?

He was sane, he set an example. Now,
as I read the poems, I find those same politics
both nostalgic & to the point.

What will I change—
if I put my crazy-arse shoulder to the wheel?
Is the answer: "In this vassal state?"

Or
"You should have thought of this earlier"?

Leave a record, like Whalen did,
of clear perceptions. The avowedly
political—Naomi Klein, Tony Negri—seem no

nearer the mark, tho fun to think about, think
with. Negri, so systematic, abstract, & wishful.
(The 'Multitude'—what a category! How do I join, ha ha.)

The overweening confidence & blindness of

think-tank America: the End of History.
Self-deluded—& the rest of the world knew.

(Cheney, Rumsfeld, the others—*Pal,*
we make history!)

A century
of Interesting Times. More. Beginning when?
1871? 1789?

The innocence, & the percipience,
of my artistic heroes seems so touching,
even their blindness. Manet O'Hara Coltrane

—loons like de Chirico—the Germans, Kirchner
Kokoschka, Adorno—Christa Wolf. Did they each sit up,
as I do, in bed—a sleeping other at their side—

writing, nodding off ... ?

The fan is going & blows my page occasionally,
though I have weighted it now with *Heavy Breathing*,
Whalen's orange-covered volume,

with its wonderful drawing ... that is too smart
to date much, really. Then one day it will date
suddenly—the ironies, the humour, the seriousness

will cease to register—a fallen, a trashed
civilization. I hope not. Tho Whalen of course
could live with it. Less tied to this world than me.

I *like* life. I like 'the continuing story', anyway,
& will be unhappy about it, the rupture. Will

the rest of my life prepare me? ("Check the serenity!"

Ha ha ha. Dreaming?)
My body, turning, in some future.

Now I read this 24 hours later, & rub Cath's
beautiful shoulder. If I "love life"

why haven't I had one—like Whalen did?
Tho I must've—mine's all <u>gone</u>, right?
In fact I don't know much about what Whalen did.

I seem to have spent mine day-dreaming—or thinking 'hard'
about music, blues & jazz, & art—& making jokes & quipping
& making poems out of it. The women

I've hung around have kept me sane. (A few were
'nuts' — but I was nuttier.)

People just want to be happy? The big,
noble notions
exist, it sometimes seems, as 'a caution', to 'ennoble'

lives

with their 'perspectives'. Rembrandt, for example,
those terrific self-portraits—*pathos, self-knowledge ... the rest.*
Dignity & failure—et cetera. *Yes,*

but let fifteen minutes pass,
& he's having a banana.
Or is that me?

A rollmop, then.

Cath reads an old favourite, laughs occasionally,
reads me bits. The fan churns,
noisily. Tho we don't notice. The night cooling

after a day of 42 & another of 37. Cool tomorrow,
at 27? 24? A small list of things-to-do builds.
My first week back at work.

Write to Sal, draw my hand
or wrist-&-watch, stuff to edit, CDs to copy
for Michael. I recommend to him

Floyd Jones: 'Tore Your Playhouse Down'
how the song rolls so casually—solid, unfussed
the solos played on top of each other

a wonderful cacophony (Fred Below, Otis ...)
The drawing—for Nick—illustration to something
he'll print. *Sal*—after 20 years—to be

evicted from her flat. A view I love. She must, too.
'Sydney'. Sydney as an idea. Slessor, Cossington-
Smith. Not that I care much about them: it is

Sal's harbour view suggests them.
At last someone wants to charge real rent.
(The old owners must have died?—or sold up?)

It will be weird if she moves somewhere I don't know.
West, I guess.

           A week later I have edited things,
Photocopied my arm—preparatory to drawing—
these are the easy things. Not written to Sal.

Tho what's to say? You have to say something of course.
Very likely she is ready for change. Regretting
the view she will lose—but impatient with the place

now the move is on. She was always something
of a Futurist. One pictures her beautiful, goggled head
hunched forward to the sights of a WWI Fokker,

or leaning low & forward on a 1930s motorbike. Laurie jokes
that I should send the T-shirts to Les Murray,
they are so big. On different sides of the planet

we smile at the idea of Les—wearing the Brainard
T-shirt, a graphic proclaiming a reading. For Ted Berrigan,
for Joe Brainard & Anne Waldman. ("Oh, boy!"

says Nancy on one, "a Poetry Reading!") Laurie's
new book is out. Fingers bent,
curled over, relaxed, I draw my left hand, held

palm upward, & the wrist. My plan is to get it right
then copy it quickly with a firmer pen
& add the watch-band. Nick requires an image

—with which to feature a particular
bright red—& a poem, against which the drawing will be
set. (A poem I wrote years ago—

that Nick found & likes. I like it, too,
so why not?) Weeks have gone past. Unchanged, the world
continues—tho shifts occur, indeterminate. The

one stability is a US stalled, awaiting the appointment
of the next incumbent. Moves will begin

when he is sworn in—the slide, the counter-measures,

the moves of Russia, India, China, Europe.

Though it's been non-stop 'interesting times',
most of it, in my life, has been going on elsewhere,
a pointy end far from here. For me,

no military service, no economic disaster.
My luck runs out?
'Blues For The Girls', 'All Blues', 'Mary's Blues'—

names I consider

for a new book, 'Mary' being Mary Christie—
but it's also an early Coltrane tune—& really
I would like it dedicated to Cath & Anna, the women

in my real life. Mary,
an old friend—in India now—in *Japan* for
the last seven years. More. I lived in her house

in Westbury Street. *The Westbury Street Poems*—
once a title I hoped to publish.
I'm sitting here in Cork—the bar, not the town.

(Write to my Irish friends.) Joyce, or Joyce's father, was
pleased to have
a painting of Cork, painted on cork, apparently.

Amused, I guess, at the finality & nominal closure
of the pun:
What's that? 'Cork.'

I find most puns shit boring, but still more so
the declaredly learned—discoursing
on their own 'delight' in them,

as if puns were naughty, & daring, & confirmed
their membership of some club—a kind of unofficial
High Culture Mensa. By the same token, I hate intellectuals

going on about Sport.
Why am I talking of this?
I don't know.

So, here I sit in Cork, time running out, luck running out—
thinking about titles—tho I can't make up my mind, &
writing them down means I can forget again for a while—

& think about art criticism—*write* some at any rate.
That is what someone wants me to do. And I'm 'on to it'—
I tell them. (I've done the drawing, meanwhile, & sent it off—

my wrist & hand—looking not too deformed—tho not
resembling exactly mine—which could be *really* satisfying.
Like 'Cork'. *My own hand* by my own hand. Is that it?)

The letter to Sal is written, posted. I think it felt
too weird—shifty, dishonourable—to write here about
maybe writing—& then not get it done. I tell her

about my picture of her as a Futurist. The
close-helmeted figure, in goggles—coming from
a Lina Wertmuller film—tho which one? In it

the joke Fascist—lantern-jawed—dumb machismo type—
speeds about, aerodynamic—
acting out his picture of himself as he does.

Tho who am I to talk? (Not exactly lantern-jawed,

not exactly machismo—tho—like a Fascist—seemingly
a little down on intellectuals: *When I hear the word "pun"*
I reach for my revolver! Yike!)

Mimi The Metal Metal-Worker.

My father's war—the second, 'world' war—was an odd one—
significant in his life—along the *Some Came Running* lines:
he was young, free (single, at least), he joined up

not to fight so much as to travel—
waiting for call-up would mean permanent duties
in Australia, & call-up seemed inevitable. My father

joined, hoping to see the world. He would have, too—
except he & his friend proved such a combination
on the 25 pounder the generals kept them home,

for permanent display. (See that tree on that hill,
says one general to another. I have a pair here
who can take it out first shot! Bolton! Nicholls! Load up!)

(Or so I imagine.)
Dad was stuck here
as his regiment—regi*ments*—would ship out ...

to New Guinea, Africa, the Middle East. My father

took increasingly long vacations AWOL & was
regularly punished. *Why did you do this, Private Bolton?*
Because I could. *I see.* From that period of his life,

a kind of paradisal time of boredom, fun, camaraderie,
he had endless stories, that I heard endless times
& can remember & would like to hear again,

hear my father tell them. Tho he's gone. Time
having run out. (Me, my
watch, & I.)

Cath will show up soon, any minute, & we'll
cross the street & shop in the markets, buying
fruit & vegetables, bread—for the weekend & the Monday,

which is Australia Day & a public holiday.
(Public Holidays, unfortunately,
mean nothing to me—*as I don't work Mondays*—

& *nobody* cares about Australia Day—this is Australia!
Altho, increasingly, people seem to. Well, count *me* out.)

Whoa! Close call. The girl taking coffee outside
is nearly collected by a young guy on a skateboard going by.
Luckily she pauses on the doorstep just in time.

Cath's arrived. (Sal,
I was going to say, liked my father,
& his stories.) My time

would have been different—Vietnam.

(Which I am grateful to have missed. Demonstrating against
        it
was bad enough—the real thing would have been awful.
My father told me—I remember—not to go if I was called up:

'Disappear,' he said.
                                    But it didn't eventuate.
It did for others.)

                    Australia Day,
at Margaret & Crab's. We sit out on their
verandah, in the dusk & then the dark, talking,

catching up, watching the street lights & moonlight
thru the leaves, listening to parties up & down,
watching young people visit. The dog, Molly,

excited & attentive, yapping occasionally,
at other times absorbed, silent.
It's hot, tho cool by now. Marg's hair,

cut shorter than usual—like a Cleopatra cut
but abbreviated, sharp. It resembles the haircuts of the girls
in Kirchner's & Heckel's paintings—& Schmidt-Rottluff's—

so severe & modern.

These models were the women Kirchner hung about with.
Girlfriends. I saw a photo of one recently—Nina Hardt—
        & was
Amazed at how modern the haircut seemed

Severe & sure, 'Bauhaus': the woman looked independent
& unfaked. Though this was *before* WWI—before

the Bauhaus, the Tingle-Tangle Girls, Dada.

It is a shock to see in the photo the real life
the painting depicted—suddenly actual,
a moment—not bent to a purpose.

Some of the Berlin scenes are pretty good.
But it's the scenes of bathing at the lake I like
& cabaret girls dancing—where Kirchner,

as well as being suckered by the women's beauty,
depicts their friendship & humour: in the chorus line
there are always two shown in conversation.

Crab points out the perfect sweetness & beauty,
& construction,
of a Little Walter solo behind Muddy.

Etta James is dead. I hadn't realised.

Perfect in her own way, a few times. An
unhappy life.

                    She will be remembered longer than me.
Unless, in the library, in the Himalayas, in 2333,
some monk decides the poetry of Australia 300 years earlier

really was interesting—& allows himself a footnote.
"Ken Bolton answered phones in an art gallery, ran a
        bookshop,
& wrote poems of wistful humour."

I see it in a small hand on an index card—
"a provincial poet in the era
of Late High Capitalism—

not much regarded,"

I have to laugh. What's that great line
of Apollinaire's,
about tossing your life off like a drink?

I finish my coffee up. (I expect
this looks like decision. Tho in fact it means
Time for work. I go there.)

Brief Life

Alone Sunday
having caught

the last of the
Ray Davies documentary,

tears in my eyes.
Still, standing

tears, not crying—
thinking, gratefully,

how good
the credits are:

silent, no image—
which gives me time

to turn the telly off
before the ads—

& smile, at some of the
English names

Rugge-Price,
somebody-Hicks.

I think, *Mervyn Hicks*, a great
footballer I used to love, his

bulk moving like
Waterloo Sunset, down

the field, dummying.

I think I saw him do it once
till he got close enough

for a drop goal.
(He missed, wonderfully)

And then I think
Susan Mervyn-Jones. Ray

has performed 'Waterloo Sunset':
life is a dream

"whenever they look at
Waterloo sunset / they are in

paradise"—Terry &
Julie, the young

clerical workers in Davies' song.
Susan was my first

girlfriend—or I
wanted her to be.

I held her once, dancing.

I still remember
the heat of her body,

the smell of her hair.
A beautiful person,

small, dark. She died
a teenager, suffering

an asthma attack
while pulling

tight clothes on
over her head

suffocated. Life
is short, Ray Davies says.

I think of Viv Miller,
last night—how good it's been

to have seen her
over these last years.

Cath rings, from Alice,
where she is.

The Todd River
is flowing it rained

so much last night.
A duck—or pigeon is it?—

sits near the river's edge.
Home tomorrow.

The dog is okay
after her operation,

Anna & Chris I
saw last night briefly—

they seem okay—

I'm not going to Penelope's
(Cath agrees).

Home tomorrow.

I play some Dave Holland,
move around the house

doing things, picking up,
tidying, straightening—

inside, outside—time
like an element around me.

The Funnies

The comics were best kept simple—
The Little King, Boofhead, Brenda Starr.
The King never spoke
& others spoke 'but briefly'
in his presence—announcing
something—this or that—
& the King would leap,
scowl or shrug,
exclamation mark
above his head.
I understood him
from an early age.
The cartoonist's
ineptitude
was essential: Boofhead's
Egyptian style
of ambulation,
his Egyptian surprise.
"The true archaic simplicity"
as someone might have said.
Arms akimbo, one leg lifted,
mouth open, his eyes—did I
ever see him sleep?—pools
of black.
The amateurish, confident
styling of Brenda Starr.
Where is that world now?
I wanna go there & roll

cigarettes, roll my own
smokes, as Dan Hicks
had it—*later*, in a more
sophisticated age—
an age that
looks back—
at the King affronted,
Boofhead flummoxed, or
Boofhead stymied,
Starr crying, or
having a thought ...
looks back, looks back,
astonished at that innocence.

II

September Poems

Postcards from the Adriatic and London
September, 2007

from Cortula

1 (Postcard home)

for Julie, Michael, Teri, Melentie

Send lots of postcards
the note said,
at work
on my last day.
I don't know
who wrote it.
Julie or Teri.
A Saturday.
I open up the shop, the
gallery, find their note.

    #
We fly out
the next day.
    #
        And here I am
after five days in London
& three in Trieste,

in Kortula.

Three days.

Angelina Jolie &
Brad Pitt
might 'be'
in the boat opposite the bar we're in.

But I don't care about them.

So, what's to report?

And is this a 'letter'
—by the by—

or a poem?

Undecided.
But the day
before me
looks pleasant —
if unexamined.

Clean air, a deferential
—a tiny—
breeze
from the sea in the bay, my
foot on my knee—where I
balance this pad & write
to you—my foot touching the table, too,

where a macchiato appears
my first this trip, my
first for years in fact.

Tho it means something different
in Adelaide:
the price of an air ticket. A
view of the blue thru pines

2 Geography

      choppy weather this morning
the water on permanent cycle
of squash, rinse, splash
(& a noise that sounds like "squulp")—
a fresh wind. Whether to
do another drawing—or wait
for these
Roy Fisher poems
to kick in.
      Tho is the Aegean
really Roy's territory? —(A correction.
The Adriatic, actually.)—
      Or not? Every sentence has to end.
("The bill."
The reckoning.)
                (The tough tone
of Roy Fisher.)
            Across the lake
a line of houses,
all dun cream with
salmon-pink roofing —
olive green behind them
in balding striations

that ascend—a grey, sharp
ridge (against
the impassive blue
of the sky), severe, forbidding;

the stark elemental
separation of colours—
whose tones say "Croatia"—

as opposed to "Italy",
"Australia", "England" or "Greece".
Roy? Jim? (James Schuyler:
for whom
the Aegean, *maybe*—the Mediterranean *rather*,
Ischia, Majorca.)

      The drawing
catches just that bit
where Cath & Gabe & Yuri swam
& Anna, too, Leigh & Stacey—

yesterday,

where the metal rails that
step down to the water
stand & gleam. Where Cath
stands now, her white jacket
against the narrowing strip of blue.
Her hands in her pockets, thoughtful.

from Hvar

3 (The rooftop apartment)

Here I am on the balcony
writing this line—the
first page
of a school
exercise book. Am I
'not very good
at holidays'?
                    Will I die
not knowing—what
a campanilé is
for instance—not knowing
'for sure'?

I have got a
considerable way
so far without that knowledge.

I think the would-be
knowing term
"campanilé envy"
made the word
no-go territory, for me.
In Italy.

But it comes back.
Washing hangs
between me & the church tower
—the campanilé, in fact—

the clothes 25 metres away
(the tower a further
seventy or so), the
enormously tall palm
curving
just off true vertical

makes an almost graphic
dark line against
the church—this last
a pleasant, distempered cream.

The palm stands a little closer
—tho further back
than the washing—
      #
two dissecting lines ,
the bellying arc
of the washing line, the
swifter, more stable
line of the dark-
trunked palm.
      #

Stains, of a 'lobster-sauce'
orange-brown,
mark the church's features—a
lobster sauce
that has been
sponged away
that clings

only in the
delineations of
carved & cut stone.
The tower
is beautiful. Each level,
as it ascends,
has more, & finer
apertures & columns—
an airier
lightening effect
while the overall
square proportions
hold:
to describe it
is too much bother,
which is not what
the church intends:
holidays.

4 The palm

The burst of fronds—
that is its tiny
head high up in the air
higher, from here,
than the church tower
('higher' even than
the mountain, a
green rugged shape—
green with patches
of grey—
further back—above it,
in uniform—today—
hazy blue

*

'burst'? it is
accurate, restful,
calming as a cliche.
As if one said
"Of course,"

5 (Here)

Arabia—'the South'—
The Mediterranean—all of these.
This is the Adriatic
—tho not far from
Italy, the South etcetera.
The Catholic, Croatian architecture
suggests even, to me, Spain,
Central America. But I know
too much & too much of it
in no detail. Know too little. Near,
Roy Fisher's poems, my glasses case,
sunglasses, a mobile phone,
another biro.
          The plastic
table cloth—over
white plastic chairs
& plastic table—faded,
almost white itself—

a pattern remaining,
of palest aqua shapes
& pale, orange-outlined
squares, circles, diamonds—

a foot or two further away.

The sun is throwing a shadow now
—as it lowers—
of my head

on these things,
the shadow even
of my biro,
my pad on my
knee

6 (Let me)

Fabulous & homely—
on the balcony ledge
in modelling clay
Anna's red stag
two inches tall
sits & leans slightly
as if drunk
against a tiny classical
head, the same size,
made from
plaster-coloured
modelling clay—its
mock-classical,
'conventional', modelled
hair—a pineapple pattern—
of tight curls. The deer's
back legs have collapsed,
comically,
so that it seems to sit down
& lean into & nuzzle
the sculpted head—to cheer it,
or to seek reassurance
against its own fears. Like
a toy from a cereal packet,
& one 2000 years old

7 ('Naphtha')

Bullwinkle—
& classicism,
gravity & the
inane. As
the poet said
"I am ashamed
of my century—
but I have to laugh"

8 (Pronto)

The phone rings …
—again!—
which gingerly I pick up
press the correct button,
it turns out, & Anna's voice says,
Hi.
"Where is Mum?"
Gelati, I say,
probably in the square

9 Views

It is one of the two vistas:

of tiled roofs,
(many aged,
discoloured,
sway-backed,
forming a soup-pea, variegated line:
a row of older
house roofs—

    against
the newer orange),

& trellis & palm tree,
  #
& the intricate
calmingly stepped
& shuffled & fanned-out
facades
of buildings

that climb
the hill,
in shallow,
flattened planes one
behind another.

The other view—
in shades of, mostly,
sandy cream—the rooves
orange or lentil—

&, pink yellow aqua,
a few walls in stucco:

A cliche but
irreproachable. The
sun, now, is strengthening.
Six o'clock maybe.

10

It even reminds me of Israel—
the castle above the hill,
the cypresses in
slightly terraced banks

11 (Two Blues)

I leave a note that says
"I'm having coffee at Mr Surly's"
& go there—
where this poem
'finds' me
staring at a sea
I sometimes refer to
as the Aegean,
tho in fact it is
the Adriatic—wondering
why I'm here.
       To
have a coffee?
Tho I have forgotten that.
(The waiter will
remind me.) To
do God's will? Not
likely. Who lives
in all those churches,
shouldn't they do it?
as they're drawing pay?
God's will, I mean.
I doubt that I am here
to reap the benefit
of my education—
"Ah, Europe!" being the
entire accrued payout.
This, this moment,
may not be unrelated—

#
I never go to Asia.
It is not a firm enough idea.
#
The nett result of
all this history, the
variegated sameness—the
brands that are everywhere
or interchangeable, *i*
Simpson, Upim, Kookai—
is to make me feel mortal
& to make the 'old' ideas—
humanity, fame, vanitas—
seem plausible. Melancholy,
& enchanted by the sound
of a scooter motor
whizzing past behind me—
or seen thru a doorway—
the silence stitching
itself together,
restoring lassitude; entranced
by the just proportion & calming
patina of a wall,
opposite the arch that frames it—
which I look thru—
(the smell of petrol, the
cheering futility of the desire
that *gunned* the accelerator
in the first place—
the going nowhere). "I'll

have a short black, please."
Then I add "Esspresso"
by way of amplification.
The waiter has shown up.
You would have to say "eventually"—
But I don't care.
The hill out there looks great
silver grey against the blue,
the blue above, the blue below

12 (Back In London)

the noise from *The
OC*. Decisions to make.
What to read? a
reading I don't want
to do. But it will
bring in money—

& I organised it,
this reading,
made it happen

'Manet Picture'
'Some Thinking'
'Mary's Blues'
'Bunny Melody' —

13 (West Hampstead)

I buy a jumper—
a top—at the Children's
Health charity shop
The woman asks where
I'm from? "Australia."

"You, too," I add—
recognising her accent
& her *look* more than anything.
She thinks she can still detect
Australian in my speech. A trace,
she says. I've only been here
four weeks, I tell her:
"I'm from Adelaide—
the more 'proper' accent."
We laugh, foreign-sounding
to the Brits around us.

III

Poem (New Way of Worrying)

for Sal & Pam, Jenny Layther & Neil Paech

Here I am in the coffee shop
I look at my list of things
to do. But which
to start on? Jen
comes in, orders—
dressed in many layers
of black—like someone
out of Daumier.
A beautiful
Japanese girl
goes past,
(short skirt,
pale-stockinged legs)
in boots, & white, woolly coat—
holding a coffee—(legs
she wishes maybe
were slenderer—
but she'd be wrong)
talking happily
to a guy as she walks,
a taller, Aussie male.
So does she worry?
I haven't seen Neil
for ages. *Should I worry—
about him?* I haven't thought
of him in ages, either.

I worry, really, about
Pam, Sal,
me & Cath.
                    The young Alison Currie
goes past. I worry maybe
about others as a way
of worrying about myself,
or disguising that I do.
Do I worry
because I'm *bored*? The
terribly handsome, terribly
continental-looking guy at
the table nearby is on the phone
—very Australian voice—
like a hitman
in a Wim Wenders movie—
Jean-Louis Trintignant—
who started
out, I think,
as a formula one driver
a name I knew as a kid—
then drove one of the cars
in a famous movie—
& moved into film
soon after. (Soon after,
I moved into poetry.)
                    The Italian-looking
guy—Jean-Louis
was French—has gone,
I see now, &

the guy he was with,
who looks more like
'the muscle' in
any good movie kill,
is pushing out
the door—where Jen
is sitting, in the fresh air
looking at papers,
mind on the job.
I feel the air
on *my* skin, imaginatively.
Yes, I could be
out there, too.
But here I am
in my regular spot,
worrying.
Now Jen moves off
wrapping
her cloaks about her—
an elegant
rag-picker (Manet),
an antiquarian
(Honoré Daumier)—
& my friend, Terry, arrives—
acquaintance really. We nod.
So, Pam, how's it going?

Train Tripping

yellowed long grass, that looks
as it did on a trip 40 years ago

to Canberra: the soft
pale, gentle hair of an old labrador

(my thought at the time)
goes by

& I remember it

& I see that grass outside.
Now.

& the song I was singing—
'Paint Your Mailbox Blue'—

a song I never hear
& always approve

—is this a life?—
thinking

of Pam & Jane & Cath &
Pam's question — as to what Cath

does alone on Bruny & my
explanation: fishing, hiking around,

dinner with Lorraine & Ian
& friends up in town

& Pam & Jane's life in Blackheath:
what they do

what they might do, &
remembering, then, Coalcliff—

but that's train trips.

Cath will be launching
her book in Hobart in a few weeks.

The film of us all
young & graceful

(the way we never knew we were)
in 1979/1980 Pam, Micky, Sal—

Laurie & me, Tom, Barb
(Barbara Brooks) I tell Pam

of Peter Sloterdijk (*Critique
of Cynical Reason*)—& of his

new book. I tell her who
he was—who I think he was.

She asks after the new Ron Padgett
How To Be Perfect—have

I read it? No,
but I'm going to & I've had it

through my shop & sold it
I'll get it again. Pam talks of

Padgett's Cendrars translations

I remember *Kodak*, a Padgett collection
of short Cendrars pieces

I associate it with the tugs
that bustled around below the window

of the flat in Glebe—Leichhardt Street—with names like
Idaho Omaha Wyoming (did

they have those names? all of those exactly?)—
they moved barges laden with wood about,

the water a deep blue around them,
the wood brown or deep orange

the tugs, of some
uncertain but evocative era—

twenties thirties forties: the mercantile
bustle & energy Cendrars saw in America

(in one of those decades probably).
Kodak was A-4, roneoed, had a glossy black

cover, with the title in 'modern'
1920s Hollywood art deco letters

a little suggestive of old Kodak
packaging. All of it—cameras, kodak,

those fonts—that lettering—*Cendrars*—old now.
I am old, & Pam. And Ron Padgett—

the American Express—is older,
Blaise Cendrars (one-armed, grizzled,

unshaven, rugged, a smoker, a drinker)
long, long dead. Do they love him in France

much, now? Blaise, George & Marie's kid,
named after him. (If this poem

is called 'Train Trip' it will match Pam's
of that name—written on this same

journey. How many years has Pam been
up here? Two, three? It seems

like a while ago I read that poem. Called in fact
'Train train'.

Maybe she wrote it soon after arriving?

She & Jane meaning to move again.
In the poem she passes Sasha's grave—so I guess

I will, tho I won't know
as it happens. Mentally she argues with him

as she passes—as she used to when
he was alive. I listen to two girls

discuss a boy who is "cute"—but "in a
good way". On the way up

a few nights back
I listened on & off for ages

to two girls & a boy. I didn't look to check & see—
but 15 or 16 I would guess. "If you

got rid of me, then you could *be with*
her—the sophistication & melodrama

of "be with her", which her voice handles
so well, 'scare quotes' ghostly, or strongly,

around all the words. She is pretty funny.
"Ghostly" of course is not an adverb,

I realise. They adopt—adopted—vaguely
wheedling complaining tones much of the time

But only as a way of ceding him
some power—as the source of statements

—of fact, of conjecture—& jokes.
He makes jokes, too.

& some of his jokes are good: the girls both laugh
but really the power is with them,

friends, lazily running thru their repertoire
of *savoir faire*, of knowledge, of

feminine fiat. I wonder how pretty
they & the boy are? Better not to find out.

A young mother, carrying her daughter on her hip
says slowly, conversationally, "Stop crying,"

& the tiny sound stops. Blacktown
station. The train is very full, of very interesting

people. I will change at Central, have
lunch in town—Greek restaurant?—

then down to
Bulli to see Kurt.

After getting off the train—Pam,
Jane—I have a typical traveller's time

at Central. A kind of shuffle
that would be irritating if one weren't prepared ...

Was I prepared? I was.
                    Then I went
to *Diethnes* where once, for a few years
at least, I ate once a fortnight. The middle

70s—a filial relationship to the owners,

Helen &
Nick, &—against my will—a rivalry, seemingly,

with the head waiter. Decades later he owned the restaurant
& was overjoyed to see me

remembering me as a best friend or at least
(some realism here) a well-remembered,

much-liked former customer. Did I try to set him
straight? I may have. Anyway

here I am. I have successfully not bought
some new shoes on the way—wonderfully lairish

& glamorous, in that Dennis Hopper/*American Friend*
        manner
& order anchovies in oil & the small Greek salad

& a carafe of retsina. Christ, I love that taste!

The place is nice still—generous. There is
the boring bastard nearby explaining

how he can't eat mushrooms. Can't those at
his table 'take it on board'? Obviously not—or

not to his satisfaction & at a neighbouring table
a big group do a lot of yelling, especially the girls

who gain the attention gratefully given to a cliché—
because everyone knows how to respond. *Bravo!*

she yells, arms over her head, attractively, because one of
        the heroes
(all in white business shirts, black pants)
        goes to the bar (!)

to order wine. But I approve—of her & him
& get back to the weird head-spaces I've occupied
        in Sydney

many times over forty years, the
        last
thirty especially—when every visit has been
        a Return.

Actually, if I weren't seeing Kurt
in just a few hours, I'd've ordered

The Diethnes Special (in
Helen & Nick's time delicious lamb on the bone

& stuffed capsicum & maybe a
zucchini or two & the most fabulous pilaf).

But it is midday. The
boring guy goes to the toilet & the two with him

earnestly discuss their divorce
& arrangements for the kids: quick, efficient thrusts,
        not much parried: they're

not scoring points but communicating. Who
is this guy then? He's not their father.

He's like one of those second rate actors
the Americans love to promote late in their
        career

to head the office in a crime show,
his ordinariness his main suit. This beige-souled

groper could outface any steady Senior Detective
—supposedly of New York, Chicago, Los Angeles etcetera—

their yellow teeth, yellow eyes, their yellow opinions
& stock phrases. (Dud pearls

drop from this guy's lips like
the print-out used to come to financial institutions,

trying always someone's patience—"Let *me*
see that!"—rips extruded tape from the machine

reads numbers, stock prices falling or tumbling, or
holding even)

("Sell amber! Buy tin!")

What future
does television have?

Have I seen its face?

The shuffle:
I ring Linda & Allan, say I won't be arriving
           after all,

don't be alarmed; ring Di & Michael
Are they in? I'm between Blackheath & Bulli—briefly—

But, as they're engaged, I explain, to their answering
machine,
& promise to ring back. Then I go & seek change

from various of the punters awaiting trains
who of course assume I'm begging

but get the correct change to make another call—
to no avail

& here I am.

Now I ring Kurt. That is, *next* I ring
           him—that is my plan

& head on down to Bulli, in
           two minds about the shoes

                    *

At Diethnes

The boring bastard—specialises
in unsurprising revelations ("I can't eat
        Mushrooms—I can eat
mushroom *sauce* but I can't eat mushrooms")
        —& in revelations that things
taken as surprising
        aren't so: Americans
landed on the moon—but they'll
        never be able to do it again
unaided. (Think of that.) Most of the
        stupefied people around him
wilt
        or fill their glass. I put
my pen thru his forehead,
        salute his dinner partners
& leave to catch my train.

(A single simple stabbing motion.)

•

September Song

for John Jenkins & Pam Brown

        "I was ...
I was born in the 70s
—no no—I was *young* in
the 70s, so the 80s still seem
new to me. Most of you, I realise,
were born then, or later,

& of course I'm so old
I might conceivably
die—before the end of this lecture,
which would be funny (tho I do not
welcome it & I am not sure
from what perspective it could
really be funny. From mine,
if you imagine the pluperfect
   regarded from the future. For those of you—are there
            any?—who
have no Latin,
that would be a little like bowling a ball, slowly,
& running quickly down the green
to see it 'arrive', to kiss the dark ball
at the other end. Is that the 'eight-ball',
or is that in pool?—the dark ball
'of death', which would effectively
end the lecture, & my life—
you'd have forgotten about me after the lecture
either way. And there is a phrase for that
& it's not *non modo sed etiam*, one I loved
in my overdetermined way: "not only but also".
&, forgotten, I can get some rest at last
(for which there is 'something', probably,
in Virgil). I who am about to die
salute you: September 26th
two thousand & ten. (Drinks glass of water,
taps mike.)"

I look out the window as the light changes
& see we are crossing water—the lake

or inlet that was Otford—&, on the
shore opposite, the house & boatshed

where Alex & Penny lived & where Claire (née Chris),
& I, visited them—& slept in sleeping bags

with the fog, that penetrated their house,
around us—in 1951? 1972? My once

best friends—with whom I never fell out
(they moved to England—

just as Gough got elected—
a kind of irony, then, they felt) who live

now in Tasmania, somewhere:
Claire will know

I remember, walking there, solo—so
how? why? drunk—

I'd drunk much of a bottle
of Marsala, thinking it might be

mescal. (I had read & re-read
Under the Volcano.)

I remember—sober, surely—
rowing with Alex & Penny &

nee Christine across that lake. Quite
a long way, to get home from dinner at a pub

(so maybe not so sober, after all)

before dark—bright, grey-white sky,

lowering cloud—& very blistered
hands. I'd never rowed before,

young, healthy, embarked.
Tho, in my case certainly, knowing not very much

Claire & me — Alex & Penn'

Diethnes —the Balkan—
where I also ate very often,

introduced by Penny & Alex.

The cook died face down
on the grill: that was the legend.

Could it be true? You would
see him there as you looked thru the window

year after year, steam rising from the onions.

I quite liked him.

I was thrown out once
(face down in my food)

Anna, Lila

Sal

'Omaha' — the tugs —

now that name always makes me think
of the beach landing at Normandy,

where Americans died—

& of cargo pants & DC2s
(& a Brainard cartoon)

(I have no idea which—
when I return to the poem.)

Nick, who cooked at Diethnes
while his wife ran front-of-house,

began as a Chinese cook down in Haymarket somewhere
in the war years.

Diethnes had very deep windowsills
on the interior of all its windows,

including the many false windows (which were murals
painted, to show simple scenes, or maybe show shuttered
windows.

Why didn't I pay more attention?) The sills
stemmed from the 6 o'clock closing era.

Drinkers, expelled from all the pubs, would come to the
restaurant,
order a basic meal, & stand with their new, legal drink

balanced on one of these tiny 'bars', the place quite full.
(I think the windows showed schematic sea & sky. I'm sure

one or two of them had a painted vase depicted
as 'on' the window sill.)

The new, young waiter—waiter-cum-cook—
took against me when I claimed not to have ordered moselle.

He'd opened it already & there must have been something
said
when he brought it back. I'd have ordered riesling—or hock,
which
         you could

still get at the time. He was very down on me, & remained
so.
It was a surprise when I met him twenty years after

& his face was suddenly wreathed in smiles. He'd forgotten.

Thank god. When I next came his son was in charge.
(Late in the 70s the restaurant

had moved across the road from where it used to be:
to it's present site—underground. History.)

Poem (What's Best)

Actually, a
week into work—after
the holidays

         (the
weekend
      ... &
Monday off)—

& finally
I am relaxed

happy even

        at what?
tho that is what's best
about it
    —that funny
flower
    that
grows outside my window
for one

associated now
with a particular friend,

Cath beside me, reading,
writing,
    kids at home, in
the back room
watching a movie

(Anna
     Gabe)
          — their
disputes so loud &
quickly resolved—
          (Hayley,)
(Alex
     —the neighbouring kid—
still a child
while the others are grown.
)
         The flower
is a yellow, creamy
white
     a bell
inside which is
a jam-red
stamen

     enough
to point up
the translucent white
surround.
         The bush has
sometimes two or
three flowers—
usually one, or none—
and not always open.

Cool weather, after a week in the 40s
the breeze moving through the room

via the windows

opened out
—into the yard,
the street—

The street-light—

moonlike,
(except that it is
always there—& like
a book design you
hardly notice)

(a streetlight

on the cover of a
book by Celine, in fact.

That I
had once.

Do I have it
still?)

I think 'moon-'
(rather than 'street-light')—

until we
go to sleep,

and then it
peers in
—*too bright*—

so unvarying it is
not the moon—

though I go to sleep. No
mozzies tonight. My little
new fan, secondhand, a
Hecla (*"By Hecla it's good!"*
their slogan in the 60s). It
runs — silent.
                    The lines,
of Cath's—pages
of type,
held up in front of her—

they parallel the broader
black & white
of the top she wears

(—bought in Italy,
knitted).

                    My feet
are bare, uncovered,

on the bed, the
bottom sheet a
pale *crème de menthe*,

the top one *a 'scrawl' of
white cotton*—from
the days of heat
before—how it looks now.

Cath puts out her light—
just me now & the benevolent
streetlight coming thru the bamboo

darker cloud
massing near the moon,
the wind coming up
to rustle the bamboo
tinkle the distant wind chime in the kitchen

then I go—open or close
windows, drink a glass
of water—
look,
from the bed, for the streetlight,
the moon—will
one have supplanted
the other?

IV
(ALL NEW TUNES)

SPIRITS

I play a little
80s Lou Reed—*Legendary Hearts*—

sentiment
& compassion,

to get me serious.

— It takes so little? —

And drink a glass
of Melentie's mastika
— a kind of ouzo
more or less.

& I've
got the mood (!)

but by proxy, as if it had
                        not 'arrived'

though it is
available —

on tap

& I
use it —

reading some poems,
attending to them,

making
corrections, changes

& that is life
you use it

you can't hold on

The way one translation
of Apollinaire's 'Zone' has it,

"Your life
that you toss off
as though it were a glass of spirits"

A glass of spirits — & bed!

It is late
but not too late,
the air is mild. Cath
reading still.

In the (large, abstract)
painting this poem
would like to resemble,
lines, colours,
             shapes,
styles or modes
or manners
             of painting,
co-habit—

with space,
to live or breathe,

beside each other—

something made up
of Micky Allan,
Kurt Brereton,
Whisson & Fitzjames
(Michael's *Optikon*, say,

showing
much of Darlinghurst,
blocks & blocks of it,
rooves & streets,
including the street
where I almost fancy
I can see the restaurant
I ate in for years
where they threw me out once
asleep before
my raznichi.
I was aghast,
how could they?
Nick & Helen at
Diethnes were never
like that, tho I didn't
test them they were like
parents. "Where is
your girlfriend tonight?")—

lines, colours, etc—
tho one, one of them,
must organise the rest,
                the others?
or can large aesthetic

continental shelves coexist,
in *detente*? They
can if I say so.
The dripping, fluid shapes
of Whisson
indicate 'Gorky' & then
'childhood'—the mill
there was no mill
in my childhood—

creeks & grass
& green declivities—

where I pictured,
I remember,
my future wife—
seated injun squaw-style
back to me in browns
beautifully cut hair
feminine gentle stylish
a large colour-chart
across her knees—
the feminine task
of deciding style—
& so unlike
the brazen hussies
I chased after—
demure, modest, elegant—
(*pace* Deborah, Lila,
Lorraine)—& in fact
they weren't hussies &

I 'chased' no one.

She was a model I saw
in an advertisement,
paid to look that way.

Look feminine!
"How?" the model
must have thought,

"I *am* feminine,
aren't I?"

—an ideal I bought into
(& Cath, of course,
does occasionally push
furniture around,
considers colours,
considers the magazines,
& is, yes, elegant

)
Spirits.

Photos on my wall—
photocopies mostly,
blu-tacked—
many I notice
            only when they go awry

& need 'a-rightening'

& pressing hard
in their corners,

where the blu-tak
hides, good still.

Some I see
regularly & notice:

the pic of Julie & Richard
beautiful, magical people
— so the photograph
testifies — photographed
at night, lit strongly,
the street dark —
coming to a small
opening of mine,
Richard a gilded youth,
Julie, girlish, a tinkering
impish angel
or witch maybe,

in this photo,
hiding, her head peeking
round the corner —
at me,
or whoever was
taking the photo —

Beside it, the picture of
her on the phone
at the office

All these people
Pam, Laurie

Richard   Jules

figures who have witnessed
my life
                & understood,
estimated it, more
realistically
than I

(Laurie's records
of Coalcliff
                — where I have none.
'Not looking'
        at the time

means I can't look back
tho nostalgic

am I? ever? always?)

                #

A burst of Nino
Rota music as
I look again at
Richard & Julie

— the final scenes of
Nights of Cabiria

urchins in the woods,
like bad fairies,
mock the heroine

                #

Anna & Chris observe
a sequence of events
from their place
at the front window
of a restaurant,

that is totally Fellini—
awful, really—but magical:

Surfers Paradise.
A bus shelter
where two girls
wait for the bus
in to the city—
a Saturday night,
very short skirts,
cheap jewellery.
A boy happens by
& accosts them, eagerly,
do they want to come
to his party tonight?
His birthday? His
twenty-first.
Lots of alcohol provided.
It will be great.
His Dad, he tells them,
thinks he is 'one sick cunt'.
He eyes one girl
particularly, much
to the consternation
of the other girl

who thinks she is
the prettier. He
drops his bottle
which smashes
on the ground.
Drops & does press-ups
in front of the girls,
lapping at the vodka. The
girls will be
impressed by his muscles.
His shirt is off.
Another friend
rocks up. Will *he*
be coming? The girls
get on the bus, one a little
regretfully. Some Japanese people
walk by & the boy
curses them at
length & loudly:
get out of Australia, basically.
The new friend says, No,
he is going in to town,
to have a *good* time.
Wrong answer.
The birthday boy
curses the chum's

                       retreating back.
Then heads off.
Stage empty.

Maybe For You

Now a sackbutt, reader, is a violin,
& I tell you this, & you nod
having suspected as much—
one type of reader does—

or you don't,
being another, a second kind of reader,

& having
known all along—

& wonder
Why do I tell you this? Will violins be my *thing* in this, this poem?

Or you grimace
—snarl—

a third response, knowing a sackbutt is not a violin,

or—more liberally—mutter "For you, bud"—
as in *Maybe for you*— & wait,

you third type of reader,
to see what will be made of it.

Let us leave the *first* reader—
who is lost, was lost before maybe, & is no wiser now—

& the second reader seems somehow hostile,

& the *third*—my type of guy, my type of girl—*Third type of Reader,
I am lost too!*

All those readers—what to do—but watch them
stroll away,

the third reader strolls, the first wanders sadly,
disconsolate not to know what a sackbutt is—

& nor do I, though I was never concerned
to know particularly—yet this

... seems somehow '*at my door*', '*down to me*',
whatever the phrase.

        And the second reader seems, furiously,
ALMOST ABOUT TO TELL ME *WHICH*,

but thinks better of it, &—'furiously'—
makes off around the corner—

then
reappears.

        No, it is John Jenkins, fellow poet —
a little put out at this sudden loss of readers.

John fixes Reader One with his gaze
& addresses him, politely, *Are you,*

perchance, a 'reader of books'?
How inviting—flattering—I see the reader pause—

& Reader *Three*, even,
look on thoughtfully—

as John begins, knowing, I am sure, the true nature of a sackbutt—
unlikely though to begin just there.

Baroque, but not remote, that is John, *thoughtful*
but not abstruse, except as a game

—in which he would not risk
to humiliate the reader, piss off

Reader Two with deliberate misinformation,
abuse the nimble mind of Reader Three.

(Reader Two I can do without—
personally—though I am very much

that *same kind* of reader, am maybe unwilling, merely,
to accept their blame—

Reader Two's "fury", remember?—
It was just a poem.

But "just a poem",
that's the very attitude ... etcetera.

I hear Graeme Rowlands' voice, warming to its task—"We've lost
Reader One, injured, hurt,

not willing to trust, easily, another poet,
not willing to trust

their own real *needs*—

for *verse*, poems with a *proper subject* &
striking, original imagery;

Reader Two was plainly better informed," Graeme continues,
"& not to be trifled with;

and Reader Three ...
is here"

—has she, or he, come
back?—

"to see if you will tell them
what a sackbutt *is*."

I thought they knew.

"If this is the same poem I was in just a moment ago," says Reader
            Three,
"it was *you* who said I knew, *not* me. (I take it I am Reader Three?)"

I hate sarcasm. Rowlands was bad enough.

In *this* scenario (sketchy, admittedly)
we seem to be standing near a table

covered with paper cups,
in each or most of which

are deposited coffee granules, tea-bags
—& an urn is steaming—

this is a conference—

though the overall scenario ...
(sketchy, as we said before—

a scenario "fictional" would not so much
describe as *explain* ...)

                    the scenario

is discontinuous. But getting
less discontinuous, you'll admit.

For instance an ordinary suburban street
constitutes the corner

Reader Two disappeared around
—nearly knocking into John, who reappeared,

a seeming poetic second wind,
coming the other way,

& nobbling Reader One,
who, when imagined walking away,

stumbles almost 'blindly'
beside a river or an empty public space —

the less frequented entrance
to a park or garden, say—

& in
slightly more autumnal weather.

Weird—three *alternative* backgrounds.

Anyway!
Reader One tends to appear (mostly)

in middle distance, small, & shrinking further.
Tall trees loom overhead, emotive green shapes,

poplars bend near him—her—them
—this reader.

In *another* scenario—one l had not even dreamed about—
they will be disconsolate, distraught,

their shame or dissatisfaction causing a loving partner
(& something of a reader 'themselves'

—male or female, straight or gay —
bi in fact—

though this is 'known'
—let's nail *something* down—only to their mother ...)

causing them
to spend a troubling night ('them'—

perhaps both of them—but not Mom)

consoling the *evident*—i.e., evidently dispiriting—grief
or anxiety

that assails their partner (unfortunate Reader One),
in such a way

that they feel
(desperately)

'shaken'
in their belief in their own sexual efficacy—

Am l unattractive? am l worthless?—
& suspect, even more alarmingly,

that their partner may themselves be bi-sexual,

& to have recently discovered it,
& to wish now—or soon, tomorrow—

to *change their lives together—*

based hitherto, as they have been, on one person's
not knowing,

& on the other person's secret.

So Reader One evidently has real concerns—

whichever one of the two Reader One *is*—

& it hardly matters
for my purposes, or yours if you're following me—

because you're a skilled reader, with
'time on your hands'.

((Much time? Do you have
   time for this?))

Scenario One, the opening line,
was a lecture, I think.

One looked up as if to a TV screen
placed high, in a pub or cafeteria,

to see—
a 'talking head'!

(Not my head. Not my voice.
Not the head of Rowlands)—

The head of the Literature Board!
In fact, the *head* of the head

of the Literature Board!
That fool!

in a quiz show, rabbiting on,
about a musical instrument.

Reader Two seems to be a contestant,
tense & peevish—

maybe this is usual with Reader Two—

in a mustard shade
of cardigan, or twinset, finger on the buzzer,

the sort of person you hate
for knowing the answer to the Question,

faintly overheard, will be ...
"sackbutt".

           Bassoon?

30.II.12

What am I going to write here?
Something, I hope. A year
or so since I last launched out

in my usual spot

and stopped, because *I didn't
want the usual*—which
after all this time with
nothing else happening
I miss. I hear
a high-pitched scattered voice,
look up,
& see an image that makes me think
"I wonder how X
is going?"—someone
I haven't seen for a while—
a blonde woman sways
distractedly, near the till,
asking a question. But not
of me. I think she is enjoying
the air-conditioning, the
sudden sense of choice. Her relief—
at the prospect of rest.
My walk here
blocked for a moment
by a girl—ex-
pensive shopping bags in
one hand mobile phone to ear

in the other—so that I thought briefly
How can anyone bear
to appear so girly? Realising
by reflex, that HOW CAN ANYONE BEAR
TO WALK OUT LIKE HIM? (say)
is a question
some woman might ask
with regard to me—
dressed, after all,
"like a styleless yak",
to quote Paul Keating
(not a woman, tho women
liked him. I liked him).
Maybe she has something
great in that bag,
the girl,
that on another day
I will applaud,
registering a kind of intelligence
I don't have or
rarely access. Lunch hour—
& *Tempo* seems filled, nearly,
with women, mostly older even
than I am.
A free concert, maybe, in the offing.
The Adelaide String Quartet
resides out back.
Soon I will hear a bell tinkling,
announcing the doors' having opened.
This building

was originally a
movie theatre, revamped
a few decades back—
the vast space within
is roped off from where I sit,
its cavernous gloom
occasionally receives
a figure carrying
a violin case
or double bass—
or these flash floods
of the elderly, or
sometimes, school children.
I look about briefly—
too blind, in this light,
to read the paper—too blind
with these eyes, is more the case:
an eye operation in
10 days time.
                              After which—
all will be revealed, maybe.
I hope I am not plunged-in-darkness—
never to see that girl again,
for example, in her
short summer frock
of dove grey, telephone
to her ear, moving dreamily,
an image, now, I love—
or these people—
or the delightfully styleless yak

I see amble past ...

& whom I join, my lunch
(half) hour up—(gone?) ((done?))

II

'X' was someone smarter than me
—in most respects
that count—thin,
drank a little too much,
coped, made a difference, as they say.

Fewer Pages—A Review

Fewer pages left—
in this pad I found—
than I thought.

—Not a metaphor.—

"(W)e've come to put our trust in suspicion"

says a canny review
in—the *London Review of Books*—

accurately shafting Alex Katz's innocence,
his having (finally, it becomes clear)

bitten off less than he might have chewed.

I like him—but agree.
I wonder if—like him—I have, too.

I always liked Katz. Tho it was clear
—*was it, always?*—they were not quite enough. The
emptiness was ... "a little empty".

Bored, rich, the shirts too clean & pressed
(& 'Beach Boys-Pat Boone')—

characters preppy, bland,
unashamed, too—

a quality, this,
the paintings held positively—

derived, says the reviewer,
from Manet &—further back, Velasquez—

or Milton Avery
(a possible first instance)?

Now, they *were* empty
(the Milton Avery)

their colour might
also have been of note,

to Katz—a tip, an influence?

The books I'm reading, for various
reasons all halfway thru

—Sloterdijk, Roussel—one too
thoughtful for my current mood—

the other hard to read
except in the best light, *but funny.*

Susan Sontag I could pick up—
her journal, the second volume—

& drift back to the sixties,

my seventies. That is, 'the sixties' occupied
my *nineteen*-seventies.

Pam's recommendation—*Panegyric*—
at work,
where I take it
& read at lunchtime:

so amusingly declarative &
calculatedly 'insolent', harsh, firm,
cheerful (cheerful 'in despite'
of things).

Not very Alex Katz.

Too Gallic for the *London Review
of Books*.

A snotty reviewer
damns Zadie Smith for
—pointlessly, he says—
focusing on guilt
at achieving a degree
of middle class status. (Hard
to please the *London Review*.)

And then he ends: *Still, it
may be her best book*.
                    'Take that'?

I sit with Pola for a bit.
Her doggy head absorbs a great deal
of massage & scrunching & stroking.

She rests it on her white paws,
wet, I see, from wading in the pool,
which she does
every so often, because it's there.

Guilt might behove, or complicate
a Katz character,

but I don't want her to feel guilty. (Do *they*?
Katz's characters?)

The fish pond
is an amenity
she should use.
                    How she sees it.

And we are amused.

                    And I write this ...
because I can
& have time, suddenly, free—
a review written—that I dreaded—
days early!—
                    a busy week
thus prepped,
so my day off becomes
my 'day off', &, like a Katz character,
what to do with it?
Like Debord, sharpen
an axe or two?
Or like Manet—whose
Sunday sailors
sometimes were given
to wearing striped shirts,
straw hats—& hung, for comfort,
with the picnic basket

(but his 'Impressionist phase'—yes?—
he probably affected the carelessness.)

(Maybe not: should Manet be
Oskar Kokoschka? No,
much as I like Oskar K.)

One prefers the anxiety
of the woman & daughter,
near the train at the Gare St Lazare:

more stripes, but anxiety
in buckets.

#

"One prefers"—
& I am one with that one.
How about you, reader?

#

Guy.

I heard an awful story once—
from the Children's Court
or Family Law—the judge asks,
And what is the child's name?
Gooey, comes the response.
Gooey? Yes, your honour.
How do you spell that? G. U. Y.
Judge nods.

Like the *London Review of Books*
I wonder—well, I *might*—how
did I get so middle class? And
how middle class, exactly (rather upper,
rather lower?) & how do I feel
about it?

Though I do not wonder.

                      The defining
middle class anxiety
might be
about becoming *no longer
middle class—losing the money.*
I will find out when I quit work:
A life not devoid of surprises.

I am not middle class enough,
for the *London Review of Books.*

Only an *Australian* this poor
would buy it. That's a thought.

(In England I would
'know my place'?

Ha ha.) In fact, I 'scarcely' buy it:

they write, begging for money.
Pam gets me a free, 'guest', or
'trial' subscription & they write
testily to her—
that their gift subscriptions
are *not for* repeat
but for new *readers*: they have
seen through "Ken Dark Horsey"—
tho they will "honour
the subscription".

Another offer from them—

is addressed to me as Fran Daddo.
But I refuse, as Fran, to subscribe.
I plan to join next,
via Pam,
as Kenneth D'Accorsi.
Will my luck hold?

The current issue—just when
I am about to throw it out—

suddenly becomes interesting.

You think it's lame
& then it isn't.

My ideas about Katz
shift and settle slightly—

I remember the extreme
bleak serenity of some—

a wow factor associated
with Abstract Art—the paint

"as good as it is in the can".

Frank Stella? I remember
the intake of breath,

the Katz blues, the reds—like
gifts.

(Like compensation for the
emptiness—which they ask us to understand.)

(Sad, troubled pretty pictures.)

NOTES

2.12.08 for Philip Whalen—"Here it comes again, imagination of myself"—the line is Philip Whalen's.

Brief Life—hardly an account of Merv Hicks' career & nor an adequate remembrance of Susan Mervyn-Jones. The point about the Todd River, as many will know, is that it hardly ever flows, sometimes not for a great many years.

The Funnies—a poem for Ron Padgett.

September poems—date from 2007. From Dubai, London and Australia the family got together in the Adriatic.

New Way of Worrying—maybe I am conflating a few generations of Trintignants into one career?

Wakefield Press is an independent publishing and
distribution company based in Adelaide, South Australia.
We love good stories and publish beautiful books.
To see our full range of books, please visit our website at
www.wakefieldpress.com.au
where all titles are available for purchase.

Find us!

Twitter: www.twitter.com/wakefieldpress
Facebook: www.facebook.com/wakefield.press
Instagram: instagram.com/wakefieldpress

Printed in Australia
AUOC02n1449040217
282761AU00001B/1/P